Living through American History

DiscoverRoo

An Imprint of Pop!
popbooksonline.com

Living through the INDUSTRIAL REVOLUTION

by Grace Hansen

WELCOME TO DiscoverRoo!

This book is filled with videos, puzzles, games, and more! Scan the QR codes* while you read, or visit the website below to make this book pop.

popbooksonline.com/indust-rev-life

abdobooks.com

Published by Pop!, a division of ABDO, PO Box 398166, Minneapolis, Minnesota 55439.

Printed in the United States of America, North Mankato, Minnesota.

052023
092023

THIS BOOK CONTAINS RECYCLED MATERIALS

Cover Photo: Library of Congress
Interior Photos: AP Images; Getty Images; Granger Image Collection; Shutterstock Images
Editor: Elizabeth Andrews
Series Designer: Laura Graphenteen; Neil Klinepier

Library of Congress Control Number: 2022950556

Publisher's Cataloging-in-Publication Data

Names: Hansen, Grace, author.
Title: Living through the Industrial Revolution / by Grace Hansen
Description: Minneapolis, Minnesota : Pop!, 2024 | Series: Living through American history | Includes online resources and index
Identifiers: ISBN 9781098244323 (lib. bdg.) | ISBN 9781098245023 (ebook)
Subjects: LCSH: Industrial revolution--United States--Juvenile literature. | Industrialization--Juvenile literature. | Economic history--Juvenile literature. | United States--Juvenile literature. | Social history--Juvenile literature.
Classification: DDC 973.2--dc23

*Scanning QR codes requires a web-enabled smart device with a QR code reader app and a camera.

TABLE OF CONTENTS

CHAPTER 1

A DIFFERENT KIND OF REVOLUTION

The Industrial Revolution began in the late 1700s in Great Britain. During this time, many British citizens **immigrated** to the United States. With them came the knowledge and experience of Britain's technological **innovations**.

The United States had just experienced a different kind of revolution.

WATCH A VIDEO HERE!

The silk industry in England boomed with the invention of new weaving technologies.

The Revolutionary War ended in 1783. Unlike the war, the Industrial Revolution did not require soldiers or battle. But life as people knew it would change completely. This transformation would continue until around the start of World War I (1914–1918).

Before the Industrial Revolution, most Americans grew their own food and made their own tools and clothes. Machines would take over much of the work people had done before. People went from working in the fields to working in factories. They earned a wage instead of growing and selling food. They bought what they needed in stores instead of making it themselves or trading for it.

Before mass production, American flags were individually crafted.

CHAPTER 2

INVENTING, TALKING, AND MOVING

Inventors helped spark the Industrial Revolution. The first **textile** factory in the United States was created in 1790. Textile mills were extremely important during this time. Using machines for mass production made clothing more affordable. People began buying their clothes rather than making it themselves.

LEARN MORE HERE!

In many cases, the Industrial Revolution made life even more difficult for enslaved people. Those on cotton plantations had to keep up with high demand.

GLORY TO GOD IN THE HIGHEST, ON EARTH PEACE, GOOD WILL TOWARD MEN.
LIBERTY AND UNION NOW AND FOR EVER
ONE AND INSEPARABLE

Improvements in transportation meant products could reach people quicker and more easily. In the late 1700s, mechanics and scientists developed boats powered by steam engines. These boats carried large amounts of cargo and passengers up and down major US waterways, such as the Mississippi River.

The electric telegraph, locomotive, and steamboat were all world-changing inventions of the 1700s and 1800s.

Workers moved handcars up and down tracks to search for damage and make repairs.

In the early 1800s, **engineers** in Great Britain and the United States created steam-powered railcars called locomotives. Before the steam engine, train cars moved along rails by human or horse power.

DID YOU KNOW?

Before the railroad and locomotives, it could take half a year to cross the country.

REVOLUTIONARY INVENTIONS

1765 - STEAM ENGINE

James Watt's improved steam engine paves the way for the steamboat and locomotive.

1770 - SPINNING JENNY

The quick spinning of wool and other fabrics leads to a boom in the textile industry.

1794 - COTTON GIN

Eli Whitney's invention speeds up the process of cleaning cotton.

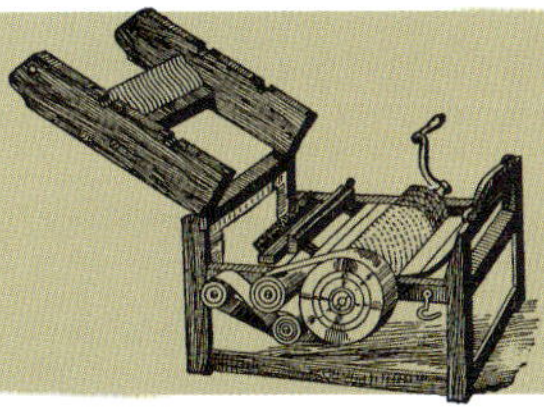

1807 - STEAMBOAT

Robert Fulton's steamboat begins service carrying passengers and light freight.

1830s - TELEGRAPH

Samuel Morse develops his own electrical telegraph and Morse code.

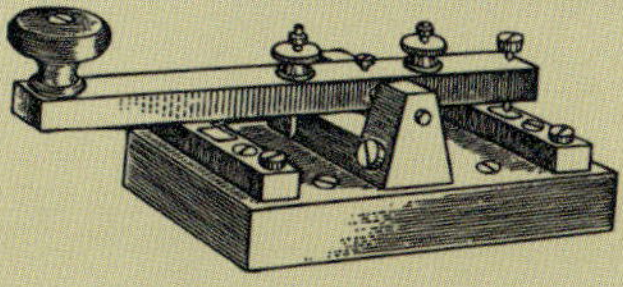

1846 - SEWING MACHINE

Elias Howe's machine allows clothes to be made quickly and cheaply in factories.

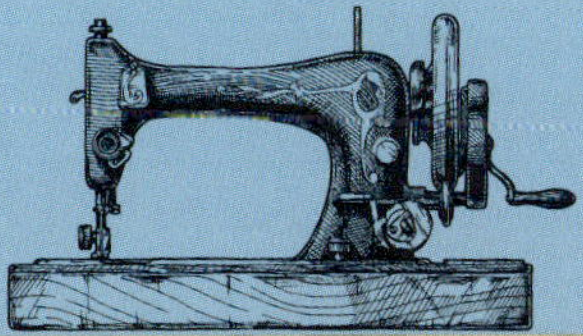

This illustration depicts lineman stringing telegraph wire along the transcontinental railroad in the 1860s.

Machines, such as the telegraph, made communication easier, bringing people closer together. Samuel Morse, a teacher of art and design, began working on his version of the telegraph in 1832. The telegraph used wires to send messages across long distances. Soon, wires connected cities and towns across the country. Americans could communicate with each other faster than ever before.

By the 1850s, railroads were common. Tracks were laid throughout the county, connecting cities. By 1870, people and products could travel by train from coast to coast in less than five days.

CHAPTER 3

A YOUNG WORKFORCE

Factories and machines flooded the country. Populations grew, especially in cities. This meant there were more **consumers** than ever before. More workers were needed to keep up with the demand for products. Two out of

EXPLORE LINKS HERE!

three people worked in manufacturing or service jobs by the 1850s. Children of poor families became a part of this workforce.

A 12-year-old girl by the name of Addie worked as a spinner in a textile mill in Vermont.

Young people had small hands to work with all the tiny parts in textile mill machinery.

Girls between the ages of seven and 14 often worked in **textile** mills. They were small enough to change spinners and **bobbins**, and they fit between machines to fix tiny parts with their hands. Workdays were 12 hours long.

Boys in Pennsylvania and Virginia often worked in coal mines. The mines provided coal for steamboats, railroads, and factories. Young workers, called "breaker boys," broke coal from rock for up to 12 hours a day. Older boys took care of the mules that hauled the coal.

Many boys worked in mines loading coal into railroad hopper cars for transport.

Some adults believed that all children had the right to attend school. Growing cities in many states began building one-room schoolhouses. This paved the way for universal public schooling, giving all children a chance to learn more skills. Most child labor was outlawed by the 1930s.

DANGEROUS WORK

Many children were injured working in factories and coal mines. Injuries often came from hands and arms getting caught in machinery. The injuries were painful and often disfiguring.

Night school was a place child laborers could go to get an education.

CHAPTER 4

CITIES AND KNOWLEDGE GROW

The Industrial Revolution changed how and where people lived. By the late 1800s, streetcars, railroads, and trolleys helped cities expand. People no longer had to live within walking distance of their jobs.

COMPLETE AN ACTIVITY HERE!

There were many ways to travel through big cities like San Francisco by the late 1800s.

Most people chose to live near those who shared their **culture** and financial status. **Immigrants** moved near others from their home countries. They ate food and spoke languages that reminded them of home.

In many cases, the government could not keep up with how fast cities were expanding. Clean water, garbage collection, and sewage systems were not sufficient. Poor **sanitation** systems

DID YOU KNOW?

In 1870, Chicago's population was about 300,000. By 1890, more than 1 million people lived there.

and cramped living spaces caused illness and death throughout the 1800s. However, these issues helped people better understand how diseases spread.

The United States experienced a large wave of immigration from the early 1800s through 1920.

Trams, carriages, and people cram the streets of Chicago around 1900.

In less than a century, the United States went from a nation of farmers to one of factory workers. The great change came with growing pains. Working conditions could be very poor. Children were often injured in factories.

Burning coal polluted the air with soot and smog. Still, the Industrial Revolution brought positive change. Goods became cheaper. People could travel and communicate more easily. Technological advances helped doctors save more lives. For most Americans, life had changed forever.

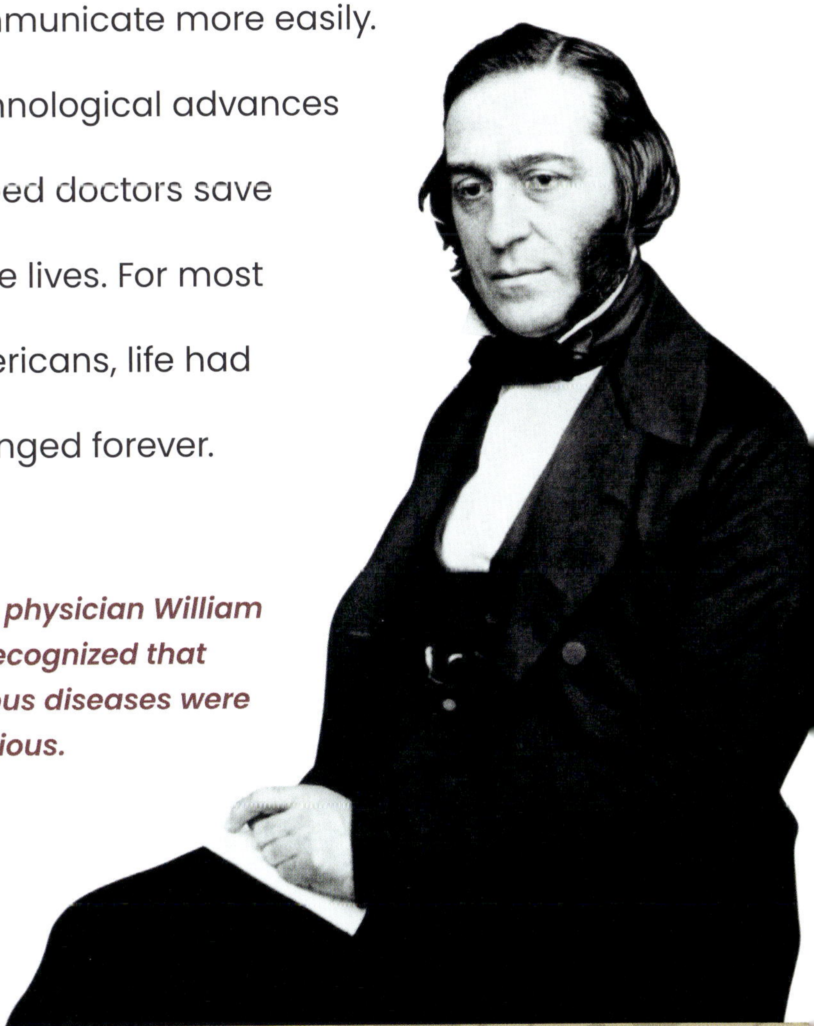

English physician William Budd recognized that infectious diseases were contagious.

A DAY IN THE LIFE

Thomas is a 12-year-old boy working in a mill. The money he makes there helps support his family.

4:30 AM

Thomas's father wakes him up. Thomas washes and gets dressed for a long day of work.

5:00 AM

Thomas quickly eats his oatcakes and gruel. It is not very tasty, but it will keep him full until lunch.

6:00 AM

Thomas begins work. The big machine called the mule starts up. It spins fiber into cloth. Thomas stands by with an oil can. He oils the tops and bottoms of the spindles to keep the mule running.

2:00 PM

Thomas returns from his 30-minute lunch break. It's time to repair one of the mule spinner's broken straps. It is skilled work that took Thomas a long time to learn.

8:00 PM

Thomas's long workday filled with cleaning equipment and machine parts, and sweeping the floors, is finally over. Exhausted, Thomas makes the trek back home.

8:15 PM

Thomas arrives home and eats a dinner of vegetable soup and milk with his family. Now it is time to get some rest before another long day of hard work.

MAKING CONNECTIONS

TEXT-TO-SELF

Is there an invention or an item that you enjoy or use on a daily basis that you read about in this book?

TEXT-TO-TEXT

Have you read any other books about the Industrial Revolution or inventions such as the telegraph? If so, what did those books have in common with this one?

TEXT-TO-WORLD

Do you think the world was a better place before or after the Industrial Revolution? Explain your answer.

GLOSSARY

bobbin — a spool on which thread or yarn is wound for use in sewing or weaving.

consumer — someone who buys goods or services.

culture — the language, customs, ideas, and art of a particular group of people.

engineer — one who is trained in the use or design of machines or engines, or in other technologies.

immigrant — a person who moves permanently to another country from his or her native land.

immigrate — to come to live permanently in a country where one was not born.

innovation — a new idea, product, or way of doing something.

sanitation — the practice of keeping the public healthy by providing clean living conditions.

textile — cloth made by weaving or knitting. A factory that makes textiles into usable products is called a textile mill.

INDEX